The Power of Relationships for Teens

TABLE OF CONTENTS

INTRODUCTION   2

CHAPTER I . RELATING TO SELF   4

CHAPTER 2. RELATING THROUGH AFFIRMATIONS   39

CHAPTER 3. RELATING THROUGH COURAGE vs. FEAR   44

CHAPTER 4. RELATING THROUGH PURPOSE   55

CHAPTER 5. RELATING TO OTHERS   63

CONCLUSION   77

INTRODUCTION

Relationships are so powerful that they can go wrong or intentionally correct, according to how we choose to embrace and cultivate them. Some are harder to keep than others, especially when rejection, bullying, and hurt are involved. So many young people are struggling due to the mistreatment of others.

Individuals dealing with self-doubt because of childhood experiences and neglect discover that moving forward in a positive, wholesome way without proper closure and peace is tough.

We are losing our young people daily through random violence and drugs. In a world today where most of us are so busy in our own lives, we do not take the time to build or maintain genuine relationships. Instead, it is the environment surrounding us, circumstances in our communities, or social media, something that keeps our time and energy consumed.

It is time to get back to love and compassion towards everyone. We do not have to walk alone on our journeys. Yes, one can get a lot done independently, but imagine what two could accomplish together.

CHAPTER 1

RELATING TO SELF

Many *people* shy away from "self-confidence" because to think more highly of ourselves than we ought, is too proud. But, thinking less of ourselves than we ought can be false humility. In between, there is an ethical approval of our worth, and that is self-esteem.

First, we must understand what love truly is before we can fully embody it. And that comes from knowing ourselves through true acceptance.

The standard for value and inner belief about self comes from how we measure our worth. Our values should be high because of how we love ourselves so deeply. Our discount is to the value our loved one's place in us, making us people of great or lessens how we see our value indeed. Because of inner strength within us, we can do far more than most have dared to dream.

Let us be honest in your estimate of ourselves, measuring our value by how much love & hope is in us. We sometimes evaluate and categorize ourselves according to how we perform, what we achieve, others' views of us, and how we look.

An honest and fair evaluation knowing the basis of our self-worth, is that our identity has been accepted and embraced.

Measuring 'self' by the worldly standards of success and achievements can cause us to overthink and view our worth through the eyes of others and miss the actual value through our own eyes. When we trust the love placed inside us, a reflection of our acceptance and virtue will emerge.

If we want to exemplify positive characteristics and attitudes, we must look through a mirror that reflects the image of love. If we genuinely want to develop our inner selves, we grow through giving because it allows love and kindness to flow more effectively. To celebrate success through these attributes, remember we are beautiful, confident, and selfless.

SELF ACCEPTANCE

Accepting self does not imply or mean giving up or staying in the same place. It is finding rest in being comfortable and uncomfortable within. Practicing acceptance means respecting the process in current conditions and acknowledging that any situation can be temporal. It is the person's perception of the matter.

Visioning a problem in terms of how it makes us feel helps us experience it as such. For example, instead of failing to get the 100% on a test, understand that this is just a tiny setback we are experiencing and use it to revise our plan for the next.

Nobody gets extremely far by being hard on themselves, especially when the criticism is unwarranted.
A positive mind pushes us forward, and when we acknowledge that we can do better, there are limitless possibilities.

Let go of negative things that do not serve us or our current situation. Continue to approach setbacks positively and brace how they make us feel.

"Noticing the feeling of such change as our understanding of the situation evolves. Learning a thing or two to prepare ourselves better for the next time will take some focus and effort but developing the skills to seek out the positive is well within everyone's ability".

"The best tool to help" is the ability always to find a way to be content and move forward. In the end, it is less about the idea of false confidence and more about self-love, appreciation of creating moments, and the ability to move forward to become who we want to be?

Name a situation that you were hard on yourself?

_____

_____

_____

_____

_____

_____

What can you do differently to feel better about the results?

_____

_____

_____

_____

SELF-DISCIPLINE

When thinking of self-discipline, try to vision operating from a moral compass or a residence of dignity. We are making decisions that will make sense rather than being sporadic and going with the flow. With that, we must process and think it through. Even being spontaneous, we still must operate from our self-restraint system.

Sometimes, to fit in, we want to hang out with the most popular, not thinking things through. We were just reacting to what is going on around our environment or surroundings at the time. When the majority is doing it, it appears like a good thing to do. However, the bravest person is the one that can take a stand in the moment that goes against their moral compass or values. What the moment requires does not make sense according to what they stand for.

How did you choose to handle a situation, when your morals or values were put on the line?

_____

_____

_____

_____

_____

_____

Is there another way that you wish you had reacted?

_____

_____

_____

_____

_____

INTEGRITY

Integrity is about being honest and authentic within ourselves first and then with others. People will appreciate that they have a sense of knowing the real us and understanding the standards we interact with, and they tend to respect more.

When building relationships from an authentic place as we communicate and engage with others, they will pretty much know if or when to invite us to certain activities.

Already knowing if we are the type that will participate or not comes because of how we have shown up in the world as our authentic selves. They can pretty much tell if you are about to engage in certain things or situations.

How do you present yourself to your friends?
(The real you or what they want you to be)?

_____

_____

_____

_____

_____

_____

Do they know what you will or not tolerate?

_____

_____

_____

_____

_____

_____

_____

_____

PRINCIPLE

Principles allow us to operate from established rules, standards, and values. For example, treating others the way that we want to be treated will be considered a principle to have.

Interacting from our principles and continuing to do so throughout our lives no matter who we meet or what situations our path may cross. It is more about being true to ourselves in the way that we choose to handle each occurrence. The rule of doing the right thing, no matter what.

How are you expressing yourself?

_____

_____

_____

_____

_____

Are you staying true to your principles?

_____

_____

_____

_____

_____

CHARACTER

An exemplary, honorable character is about showing up globally and operating from all acquired traits discovered through evolving and becoming our true selves.

We will begin to form great quality features so that the world may see our good nature.

Our character will eventually evolve, no matter what we are involved in or who we are around. It will genuinely guide how we treat ourselves and others even when we do not think others are watching.

Our character still being shaped, defined, and spoken upon; will be evident by the way we walk out, not the best times but some of the worst times that we may endure, and that's how people get to see.

Character says a lot about an individual and if that she/he is someone that we want on our team in business or friendship.

Partners going through life together knowing how we will be able to count on them or not based off their character.

Name some positive traits about yourself?

_____

_____

_____

_____

_____

What would you like to improve?

_____

_____

_____

_____

_____

GOODNESS

Goodness is a state of being. A heart to do good towards self and others. Sometimes we feel that being good and kind makes us appear weak, especially when we have gone through hardships.

It seems like with family dysfunctionality, being picked on and talked about is hard to overcome to function from a place of goodness and allow it to be the constant state of our heart still.

Remember, everyone has problems to face. Try not to let it change the core of our hearts, becoming bitter and angry; instead, try to learn and grow from our experiences.

What do you give your generosity too?

_____

_____

_____

_____

_____

How do you share this goodness with others?

_____

_____

_____

_____

_____

_____

VIRTUE

Learning how to show up in the world with a positive perspective on what you see, hear, and do. Having a mindset filled with hope, love, and faith that things are good, can be good, will be good, and contribute to this result.

What do Virtue mean to you?

_____
_____
_____
_____
_____

How would you share it with others?

_____
_____
_____
_____
_____

"SELF-CARE"

When asked, most young people and some older adults, what self-care is, their minds think of outwardly things like getting their nails done, haircut, and exercise. Beautiful things like that, but we often forget that it initiates from within.

Self-care can start from affirming words that we speak over ourselves daily, the values and morals we stand by, and being true to our authentic selves.

We do not have to operate from a false sense of confidence by representing outward appearances but finding a balance in everything is self-care.

How do you care for yourself?

_____

_____

_____

_____

_____

_____

_____

_____

What would you like to add for more self-care?

_____

_____

_____

_____

_____

_____

SELF-ESTEEM

Self-esteem is believing and speaking proudly over ourselves than others. Our own words are the best form of communication to have to esteem ourselves higher.

Ones belief about themselves will establish higher self-esteem such as, " I am loved, " I am enough" or lower feelings of doubt and shame. Self-esteem is our perspective of our own worth.

What words do you use to describe yourself?

_____

_____

_____

_____

_____

_____

_____

SELF-RESPECT

Having respect for ourselves is essential, so before deciding to do something that can jeopardize our view, weigh it out to see if it makes sense or is worth compromising.

What will it cost, what do we have to give up, what are we saying yes?

What do self-respect look like to you?

_____

_____

_____

_____

_____

_____

_____

_____

_____

_____

SELF-REGARD

Holding ourselves accountable to keep what is
deemed valuable to us, a standard to make
decisions.

We see ourselves in high regard.
We see our abilities and talents in high regard.
We see our skills and education in high regard.

Place a high cost on what we have to offer the
world. Taking pride in what we believe in and
what we stand for.

Self-evaluation always remains fair and favorable,
seeing the glass half full rather than half empty,
keeping our faith and hope in ourselves and others,
allowing it to be our guiding light.

DIGNITY

Walking proudly with our shoulders broad & strong, head up with a smile, knowing who we are no matter what others say and do or what we must confront.

SELF-CONFIDENCE

We might not always feel confident in everything but will feel well-grounded and self-assured by attempting to keep our morale in every situation.

What is your evaluation of your self-esteem?

_____

_____

_____

_____

What words can you write down for more positive evaluation?

_____

_____

_____

_____

_____

_____

_____

_____

CHAPTER 2
RELATING THROUGH AFFIRMATIONS

Our words are so powerful; that's why it is essential to choose what we will say. Stating what we desire or trying to obtain must be affirmed daily.

Affirmations are words or sentences aimed to affect the mindset, so our behavior, habits, communication, and environment can be transformed and shaped into what we create.

Our words can take on their own belief; therefore, they will bring up related mental images to inspire and motivate us to keep going towards the goal.

The act of believing and writing or speaking about something to be true. An example of affirmation is reminding a child that she/he is smart. It can be a statement of truth which one desires to have in his life. Affirmations are practical steps not wishful thinking.

One person's dream may become the first generation of their family to attend college. Not only is that possible if they begin speaking it daily, but it will also more likely become attainable. As we affirm, then believe it, our motivation and determination pursue the steps to getting there. Whatever it takes, sharing it with family, friends, teachers, or community until someone assists with making it happen. Whatever we are trying to achieve, let it be fueled by positivity and take practical steps to get there.

Speak Positive Affirmations Daily!

COURAGEOUS	JOYFUL BLESSED	THOUGHTFUL	Smart	BEAUTIFUL GENEROUS LIMITLESS
GOOD, HOPEFUL I BELIEVE IN MYSELF	ENOUGH	FRIENDLY & A GREAT LISTENER	K I N D	IN PURSUIT OF Happiness & PEACE
A LEADER A STUDENT A TEACHER	A WINNER, DO NOT GIVE UP	DISCIPLINED SELF-ACCEPTANCE	Nice	HEALTHY
I HAVE SELF-CONFIDENCE	I HAVE self-respect		Strong	PATIENT, RESPECTFUL GRATEFUL

I AM_____

I WILL_____I CAN_____

CHAPTER 3

RELATING THROUGH COURAGE VS FEAR

COURAGE

Courage is the willingness to make a bold decision and braveness to confront disappointment, defeat, uncertainty, or intimidation. The ability to do something that one is currently afraid of is courageous strength of honor in the face of pain or misery.

Physical courage is bravery amid hardship or dealing with a bully, especially one that likes to pick a fight with us. "Ms. T showed courage by reporting the bullying to the proper authority and named everyone that was involved."

Moral courage is the ability to remain justly in the face of significant opposition, like a scandal. "Ms. T called on all her courage to face the situation."

BRAVERY

When faced with a bully, they often express their inner hurt and insecurities outwardly towards another, so it is imperative not to become a bully.

Focusing on our inner wellness allows us to have compassion for others instead of putting them down.

We can become the person who will stand up against that behavior because we are well-rounded individuals. It takes someone to be very courageous to take a stand on what is right or fair.

PEACE-MAKER

If we find ourselves in a situation, having a confrontation with someone. After talking with them and realize that we were wrong or were giving misguided information about the matter, it is okay to be the bigger person and make peace with that individual(s) so you both can move on, especially if they are willing.

FEAR

Being courageous does not mean that we are not afraid. It means that we are willing to go after our goals and dreams despite the fear. We can move forward towards the goals that we want to achieve by being brave. We may have to adjust the way that will work best for us to accomplish them.

Taking baby steps helps not to become overwhelmed with focusing too much on the big picture or finished goal. Stop comparing ourselves to others on how they navigate through their circumstances. Everyone is dealing with their fears and or struggles, and no one is perfect. Encourage ourselves with our minor accomplishments.

Then add the next step or steps, and before we know it, there goes the finished picture, and we got through all the roadblocks and fears.

Obstacles will appear throughout life but building a strategy of facing them head-on from an early age will help prepare us. We will not do everything perfectly, will not do everything confidently, however, we can do everything courageously.

The goal is not to beat up on ourselves when mistakes happen, or something did not work out the way we wanted. Own it, learn from it, then pick ourselves up from it and move forward. What we will accomplish will be good enough, mainly because it came from our hearts.

Sometimes when hardships occur, it tries to alter the view of ourselves and sometimes stagnate us from moving. We must learn how to give it our best, do all that we can, come from that authentic place within, and if it still does not turn out the way we intended, we must learn how to let go and take the pressure off ourselves—staying open to creating another way to attain it.

What are some of your fears?

_____

_____

_____

_____

_____

_____

_____

What courageous steps will you take to accomplish goals?

_____

_____

_____

_____

_____

_____

_____

POSITIVE SELF-AFFIRMATIONS

I AM ENOUGH	MY DREAMS WILL COME TRUE!
I will ACHIEVE MY GOALS!	PERSEVERANCE IS MY FRIEND! (One step at a time)
I BELIEVE IN MYSELF!	I AM An OVERCOMER!
MY SELF-EXPRESSION IS POSITIVE!	I am Loved!
MY WORDS MATTER!	I AM A GIVER!
SUCCESS begins FROM WITHIN!	I GET TO CHOOSE HOW I FINISH!
IN CHARGE OF MY own LIFE!	FORGIVE MYSELF TOO!
TODAY I CHOOSE TO BE BRAVE!	PERFECT, JUST THEWAY I AM!
TODAY I CHOOSE TO BE FEARLESS!	I MATTER!
MY INTENTIONS ARE GOOD!	I'VE ALREADY WON!

CHAPTER 4

RELATING THROUGH PURPOSE

Our relationship with ourselves and others will help determine how to discover purpose. We are passionate about doing that special thing and being a part of it for the greater good—our contribution to the world.

Life lessons from the good, bad, and ugly help reveal that special uniqueness in all of us. Uniquely designed, there is only one of us. The family, friends, community, and the world need that ability, talent, and gift that only we can share. We can be imitated but never duplicated.

Everyone should willingly explore, identify, develop, and flourish that specialty that is within them. Gain knowledge through our education, surroundings, and mistakes. Discover our strengths and weak areas, so we will not be surprised when others try to shine a light on them.

We should be striving to embrace purpose, vision, a plan, and a way to make it happen for our lives.

When ordinary people decide to reach for an extraordinary life-which, as it turns out, is precisely the kind that they were meant; is their success.

Success is not about winning a competition or sort. It is when one feels that they have accomplished their goal(s).

It is establishing a vision and plan for our lives and pursuing after it, whether the goal is a doctor, lawyer, housewife, or president. Remembering to adjust as our goals will change throughout life.

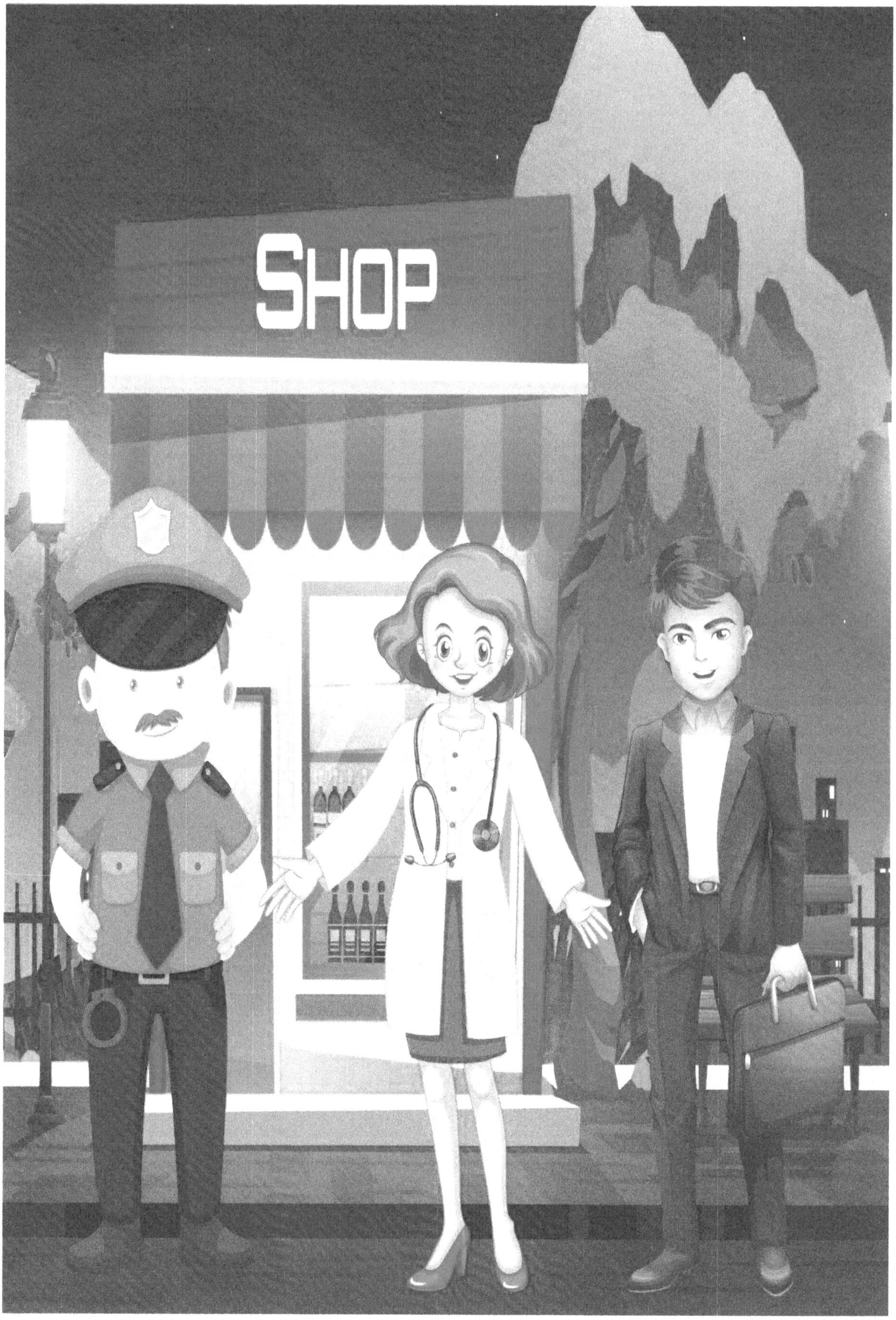
SHOP

We can only measure success by the standards that we placed inside of ourselves. Everyone's success does not look the same, so do not compare, just do us!

Our pursuit toward inner peace should be an everyday lifestyle as we show gratitude for who we are and all we will contribute to our community and the world. We develop our purpose through our abilities, passion, and study of life experiences. Through learning, gaining knowledge, and wisdom, our conditions and circumstances can begin to change. Purpose can make us feel complete and balanced by conditioning our mindset. Everything we may face in this world does not have to define us but will open another level of awareness.

All of us will fall short sometimes. If so, just get up, shake it off(reset); and keep moving forward. Do not shuffle in our mistakes too long. Self-doubt will try to use that experience to keep us stuck and give up on our purposeful journey.

What does purpose mean to you?

_____

_____

_____

_____

Would you like to discover your purpose? Why?

_____

_____

_____

_____

Write and draw what you would like to do as a professional?

_____

_____

_____

_____

CHAPTER 5

RELATING TO OTHERS

Two people can accomplish much more than one; they get a better increase from working together. If one person stumbles, the other can reach out and help, but for individuals who are alone when they stumble or fall, things can become more challenging to manage.

Do you consider yourself an introvert or extrovert and how do you express when communicating?

_____

_____

_____

_____

What ways would you like to connect better with others?

_____

_____

_____

_____

Many barriers can divide us from other people at large; Our age, appearance, intelligence, political views, economic status, or race are some common factors we may not be aware of in our everyday life.

For example, many of us say that we engage with all people but look around our environment and see how many nationalities live close that we do not socialize.

Look inside our schools, have we interacted with someone that on the outside may appear different than us. Everyone sees all the beautiful colors of race; however, love helps treat all human-kind equal. One of the best ways to stifle love is to be friendly with only those who are alike.

Let us consider the different perspectives of why division among us is still there. There is a church on every corner just about, and we will hardly come together for our communities. Instead, we compete. Do we think that one is more than the other, or have we fooled ourselves to believe that we are better? This kind of thinking is why we sometimes appear closed-minded. No matter what the circumstances are, a disciplined mind maintains balance through love and peace.

We should call upon friends and family for support with the same common purpose, building community. Love helps us look beyond the barriers to get to the unity we can enjoy. While on our journey, some of us have become complacent and harden by the cares of life.

Let's examine our intentions and challenge ourselves to see if we care for one another the way we should. We are encouraged to share our love, faith, sympathy, joys, sorrows, and hope. And when we share, we connect with others in our relationships and demonstrate our selflessness. We are to give because love has so generously given to us and each of us have different gifts, and by sharing our gifts and talents with others, we experience the full range of rewards.

FAMILY

Our families are mainly there in time of need, so they might not come around us daily, but that does not mean that we are not loved. As we mature and become more independent of our families, that may reflect less time spent together. Let us appreciate the moments we share with our loved ones and cherish them because we never know when we need them.

We should give and receive the support of others, realizing we do not have to explore this life journey alone. If we find ourselves dealing with everything alone, be careful, and make sure that it is not us that has pushed everyone away.

Sometimes because we have experienced so much hurt and rejection, we close the door to cultivating friendships. We will try to convince ourselves that we will not have to worry about being rejected or mistreated again if we keep people at a distance. Search for ones that are looking for the same common goal of friendship.

FRENEMIES

Operating from our truth allows us to walk in love even towards our frenemies and not be concerned about receiving it back. Do not let their actions change our core or essence of kindness.

We must remember how to guard our hearts while still releasing help unto each other in everything we do. Being more thoughtful and considerate to others should be another goal to achieve as we mature.

You may not be considered the most popular among your peers after choosing to walk kindly, but you will feel proud on the inside.

SOCIALLY

It is crucial to consider how we present ourselves to the world and what should matter to us. It is not about putting up a facade or pretending. Be cautious of what we are giving of ourselves on social media.

Still, sometimes the way we offer ourselves can lead to other opportunities we have not had, for a great career, healthy relationships, and friendships.

How Attitude Matters:

_____
_____
_____
_____

How Communication Matters:

_____
_____
_____
_____

How Self-Expression Matters:

_____

_____

_____

_____

Have you thought about what kind of image you
are presenting to the world?

_____

_____

_____

_____

How you communicate says a lot about you, how
would you define your communication style?

_____

_____

_____

_____

What kind of attitude do you lead with in difficult
situations?_____

_____

_____

_____

Complete Sentence Affirmation:

My relationship with_____ is the most important.

To accept me is essential to having a life of_____

_____

To genuinely love and_____ is growth and maturity on my life journey.

I was created as _____being.

Because we live in a world with other people, it is important that_____

___people can accomplish much more than one.

My relationship with others should not compromise_____.

_____designed families to provide love, guidance, encouragement, care, and enjoyment.

The foundations of healthy relationships are_____.

Continue in loyalty and kindness will find me_____with others.

One person building a relationship alone is nearly_____.

_____can keep me
experiencing some loving relationships.
_____will keep my heart
open to receiving the fullness of relationships.

Relationships with respect will
_____ a lot.
Forgiveness does not mean the
_____ is restored.

Some relationships I form,

_____.

Experiencing————————————————— can
help with how I relate to others.
My family is_____ and will be there in a time of
need.
My true friends will be there
_____.

When I believe in myself

_____.

Conclusion

Upon establishing our most potent relationship, which is within ourselves, then others, there are many opportunities we will be given, and the fullness of life will be attainable to us while on earth.

We receive characteristics by becoming a son and daughter of our loving family, culture, community, and other parts that we will establish.

Hopefully, being led by our moral compass gives wisdom, understanding, counsel, and knowledge. As we continue to walk in truth and kindness, we can pursue a balanced and fulfilled life by honoring ourselves and others.

It is so wise to keep our hearts pure and guarded for purpose. Do not allow the care of material things to keep us from appreciating the littler blessings—walk-in integrity, love, peace, joy, discipline, and goodness.

There is strength in healthy relationships with self and others. Remember, instead of ending relationships with our family member or good friend that made a mistake, go to them in love and correct it if they are willing to do the restoration work.

We are one race, humanity; let us get back to embracing one another through love and kindness. Yes, we will endure hardships sometimes, and experience difficulties that can be self-inflicted or through others but continue to stay graceful daily to always respond in the best way. Then hopefully, your relationships can remain steadfast as they evolve.

The end

Made in the USA
Columbia, SC
10 February 2023

11281855R00043